Institute Research Number 230
ISBN 1-58511-230-5

CAREER AS A

CHEF

EXECUTIVE CHEF

SOUS CHEF

TAKE TWO CUPS OF CULINARY TALENT, A pound of passion, and three tablespoons of creativity. Sprinkle in some imagination, dedication, perseverance, energy, and a flair for making magic in the kitchen. Mix together and you have the start of a recipe for becoming a great chef.

The world is fascinated by those who can dazzle the taste buds. People will go out of their way to vacation in locales that have spectacular restaurants with internationally known chefs presenting their dining creations to please the palate. Chefs guard their recipes for signature dishes the way nations around the world protect classified information.

If you love food, this is a field that offers countless career opportunities, and it is always expanding. A chef can specialize in desserts and pastries or run an entire kitchen, serve classic fare with an extraordinary twist or craft exciting new offerings, prepare cuisine from around the world or focus on culinary delights from one particular region.

There is always a niche to be explored, as is evident by the growing demand for healthier food options in the realm of gourmet dining. Food lovers maintain a hearty appetite for the next big culinary trend, and that makes being a chef rather challenging. No matter how good you are, you must keep coming up with fresh new ideas in this very competitive field.

Great cooking is an art form, and chefs can push the envelope as far as they dare, as long as ingredients and flavors work together. Using a plate as their canvas and food as their palette, chefs bring their ideas to an eager public, just as artists fill the walls of the world's great museums with their latest images. In a harmonious blend, chefs mix textures, tastes, colors, and scents.

Meal after meal, great chefs strive to reach new heights, even though some might think they have attained the pinnacle. There is always an element of surprise in every outstanding chef's mixing bowl.

The field has received an enormous boost from television programs like the Today Show and Good Morning America, which have regular cooking segments, Top Chef, and networks like the Food Channel.

Bookstore shelves are filled with cookbooks from some of the most renowned chefs throughout the world. Chefs and their recipes are showcased in all types of media, from printed magazines to websites and blogs.

WHAT YOU CAN DO NOW

COOKING IS THE ONLY WAY YOU CAN find out if a career in the kitchen is really for you. Loving food is important, but you have to love the process of preparing food. If you become a professional chef, you will be cooking every day, so now is the time to find out if you are happy doing that.

Once you get comfortable with a series of recipes, you might want to start adding your own special touches. Experimenting in the kitchen is an essential aspect of cooking. You have to develop your own knowledge about what ingredients and spices go together.

Chefs garner their culinary expertise from a variety of sources. They usually gain their first insights into food preparation while growing up, from someone in their own home. If you have spent some time around your stove and cutting board at home and want to extend that experience, you might want to see if there is a soup kitchen near you that is seeking some volunteer help. This will give you an opportunity to be in the hectic atmosphere of a busy kitchen. It is a setting similar to what most chefs face every day.

Start formal training as soon as possible. Some high schools offer cooking classes, as do some YM-YWCAs, and community and continuing education centers.

HISTORY OF THE CAREER

THERE WERE PUBLIC INNS AND taverns where citizens of ancient Rome could enjoy a hearty meal and a night on the town. The food was prepared by cooks and served to patrons sitting at long, wooden tables.

Kings and rulers throughout history have relished great food and would scour their kingdoms to find the best cooks in the land to run their kitchens.

British and French monarchs have long boasted of the culinary excellence of their chefs, though working in the British royal kitchen could be hazardous. There is a well-known story that England's King Henry VIII beheaded his chef after finding a hair in his soup. The next royal chef started wearing a hat when preparing the king's meals.

The word chef is a shortened version of the French term *chef de cuisine*, which means director or head of the kitchen. It is no secret that the French dominated the culinary scene for centuries, starting in the 1700s, and they are recognized for originating the restaurant. Most historians agree that the first eating place that resembles a modern-day restaurant was opened in 1782 in Paris by gifted chef Antoine Beauvilliers. Called La Grande Taverne de Loudres, Beauvilliers's luxury eating establishment is credited with being the first to combine the four essentials of a great dining experience. Those critical elements, according to the celebrated French gastronome Jean-Anthelme Brillat-Savarin (1755 - 1826), are superior cooking, a great wine cellar, smart waiters, and an elegant dining room. Beauvilliers believed that people should know what a restaurant has to offer, so he developed menus. He was the perfect host. Beauvilliers was said to remember guests' names and what food and wine they liked and disliked.

Marie-Antoine Careme (1784 - 1833), another Frenchman, earned the title of "King of Chefs and Chef of Kings." Born into a poor family of at least 25 children, Careme was put out on the street to make his own way in the world when he was 10 years old. He knocked on the door of a restaurant, looking for a job. By the time he was 21, he was one of the most accomplished chefs in France. He created *haute cuisine*, a style of French cooking used at the most prestigious, upper-crust eateries. Haute cuisine is known for both its elaborate preparation and its small portions and numerous courses. Many members of French high society, including Napoleon and French diplomat Charles Maurice de Talleyrand-Perigord, hired Careme to prepare meals for them. He made many of the meals served when foreign diplomats came to France. Later in his life, Careme was the head chef for the future king of England, George IV.

Georges Auguste Escoffier (1846 - 1935) modernized Careme's haute cuisine and simplified it at the same time. He was the most well-known chef and restaurateur in France in the early part of the 20th century. In 1893, he created a special dessert, Peach Melba, for a dinner held in honor of Australian singer Nellie Melba. He also named Melba Toast after her. Escoffier joined with several business partners a few years later to open first the Ritz Hotel in Paris and then the Carlton Hotel in London. He was responsible for organizing the kitchens at the hotels, and his sumptuous dishes brought in the rich and famous.

Another French chef, Charles Ranhofer (1836 - 1899), brought his culinary expertise to one of New York City's dining hot spots, Delmonico's, in 1862. He turned the restaurant into the finest dining establishment in the United States at the time. Many legendary dishes were originated there, including Lobster Newberg, Chicken a la King, Eggs Benedict, Baked Alaska and Manhattan Clam Chowder.

One of America's top homegrown chefs hailed from Pasadena, California, but actually got her culinary training in France. Julia Child (1912 - 2004) did not start cooking until she was in her 30s. Her culinary interest was sparked in 1948, when she moved to France with her husband. There she attended Le Cordon Bleu, the renowned cooking school, and studied cooking with several French master chefs. After publishing a book on French cooking in 1961, Child made a guest appearance on a TV show on the National Educational Network's Boston affiliate, WGBH, in 1962. The audience loved the way Child effortlessly demonstrated how to cook an omelet and wanted to see more. WGBH offered Child her own show in 1963, a program that soon went national.

Julia Child is considered the first celebrity chef. Though there were other chefs on television, few presented cooking with the ease that Child did. She wasn't afraid of making a mistake on the air, correcting it, and picking up where she left off. She made it seem as though, with perseverance, anyone could cook. Child was entertaining and encouraged people to have fun while cooking. Many believe Child's flamboyant, breezy style on television paved the way for many of today's cooking shows, the Food Network, and the eventual celebrity status of some of the world's top chefs.

WHERE YOU WILL WORK

CHEFS CAN BE FOUND EVERYWHERE people go to have a meal, and that list continues to grow. Depending on where they work, chefs may prepare meals for a few people, or thousands. There are top-notch cooks who work on private yachts and in spacious banquet halls. Tasty meals are served in hotels, trend-setting museums, nightclubs, cruise ships, resorts, country clubs, executive dining rooms in major corporate headquarters as well as casual- and fine-dining restaurants throughout the globe.

Big cities, small towns, theater districts, commercial centers, exotic getaway locations, or around your own corner – there are no limitations on where good food is served. A career in the kitchen can be found close to home or in far-off places.

If you like working with particular types of foods, that might guide your decision about where to work. Chefs who favor preparing fish, for example, might choose to work in a coastal community, while cooks who fancy Cajun cuisine could put down stakes in Louisiana.

The possibilities abound. Some chefs undertake special assignments, like those who travel on location with big-budget movies to cook superb meals that keep cast and crew happy during filming far away from home. The President of the United States has his own chef – a number of them, in fact – and so do many other world leaders.

It is not unusual for wealthy people, including movie stars, entertainers, and athletes, to have meals prepared right in their own homes by full-time chefs on their staff.

It often comes down to where a chef is most comfortable and happy working. The most desirable location for most chefs is a well-known "white-tablecloth" restaurant. The chefs at these "fine dining" establishments are often stars in their own right, building up their clientele based on their renowned reputations. Some chefs own their own restaurants or are partners in them. These chefs enjoy the option of preparing individual meals for adoring fans, often inviting diners to sit in the kitchen and observe the action. Sometimes they will even cook something not on the menu for a special patron.

A bigger customer base can be found in destination hotels and resorts, where people go on vacation and look for that special meal that will stand out in their minds forever. There are many chefs willing to accommodate these culinary adventurers, preparing dishes that reflect the tastes of a particular region.

Special events, like weddings, awards dinners, reunions, and anniversary celebrations, are catered affairs with large guest lists. These draw on a chef's talent for putting a wide range of foods on the table, that will please people with varying tastes.

Taking to the classroom after putting in time in the kitchen appeals to many chefs who want to share their knowledge with the upcoming talent entering the field of professional cooking. Culinary schools and colleges offering degrees in the culinary arts are always looking to beef up their faculties with experienced chefs who have firsthand insights into preparing extraordinary meals.

More chefs than ever before are donning an apron and cooking in front of a television camera. This is part-time work for some chefs, who combine it with regular kitchen duties. Others make a career out of preparing food as a show, helping to feed viewers' growing interest in every style of cuisine imaginable. Connecting with a television audience has brought fame to many professional chefs, and has called attention to their distinctive brand of cooking.

THE WORK OF A CHEF

Executive Chef

Most restaurant kitchens have more than one chef – it is a team effort. The executive chef or head chef is the boss and oversees everything that goes on in the kitchen.

Setting the tone, and directing how the kitchen is run is your most important job. All the meals are cooked using recipes created by the head chef. You have the final say on the ingredients used in those recipes and no varia-

6

tions can be made without your consent. You will also need an extensive reserve of recipes for specials, seasonal dishes, and changes to the menu – all critical to keeping a restaurant in the vanguard.

The role of top chef includes making sure all the ingredients used in the meals meet quality standards, and choosing the vendors to provide those ingredients. The head chef hires the staff and actively recruits new cooks or bakers. Your responsibility is overseeing and training new chefs.

Ordering equipment for the kitchen is done by the head chef, as is making budgets for the kitchen and its staff. Budgets have to include salaries, the cost of food and supplies, and an allowance for new equipment and maintenance.

Another important job is planning. Spectacular meals don't just happen. They spring from a chef's vision. Menu planning can be exceedingly time consuming. Menus are developed weeks in advance. Hours of planning go into choosing what will be on the menu and the specials that will be offered to guests on particular nights. Seasonal delights are introduced, and careful attention is paid to having a variety of menu items that will suit the tastes of all the guests who come into your dining room.

All aspects of the meals have to be planned – appetizers, salads, main courses, and desserts. The different dishes have to work well with each other. Tastes, colors, and textures of the foods on a plate cannot conflict with each other. The wines have to match the meals that are served. Sauces and dressings must complement the food as well.

The chef is the person who makes all this happen. The food has to fit in with the ambience of the restaurant. As the chef, you have to make the food the star attraction. Even if you cook food at an eatery that has a set menu, the ownership will probably want you to present ideas for new items that will liven up the menu.

In today's competitive restaurant world, diners are looking for menu selections that will excite them, a reason to come to your restaurant rather than another. This will test your creativity as well as your knowledge of what other eateries are serving, and what you can do to make dishes special and different.

Perhaps you want to introduce some foods that the restaurant has not been serving on a regular basis. You put pencil to paper and sketch out your ideas, like an architect drawing a new building. You look at various food groups and think about putting some fish on the menu, adding a few vegetarian dishes, introducing couscous or quinoa as an alternative to potatoes, and integrating "spa food" – tantalizing low-fat, calorie-conscious meals. Knowing when to change the menu to shake things up a bit, to infuse the dining room with some innovative creations is the successful chef's forte.

Another essential part of the chef's behind-the-scenes work is ordering ingredients. Very large restaurants will have someone – usually one of the mid-level chefs – order the ingredients necessary to make the meals. In most kitchens, this task will fall to the head chef. Ordering too much or too little food can be a very costly error. Proper ordering is an acquired skill.

Another problem is food you cannot use, at least for the moment. Sometimes you are just left with too much dark-meat chicken or fresh salmon steaks. Coming up with a clever way to use the surplus is an issue chefs wrestle with all the time.

Making time to come out and meet, greet, and talk to guests is often part of the routine. Successful executive chefs know how much this can mean to customers, how it enhances the dining experience and helps prompt return visits by regular customers. Successful executive chefs get to know their clientele. They prepare unique dishes for them, help them celebrate special occasions, suggest a special vintage for a perfect wine paring with dinner. Making their guests feel welcome, giving them individual, often personal, attention, yet never losing sight of the other guests in the dining room, can make a great chef a legend.

Promotion in the digital age has added to the busy to-do list most chefs already have on their desks. Chefs now keep in contact with their patrons via e-mail, blogs, and Facebook pages, to prompt return visits to the restaurant. Writing short messages about your latest savory creation, the story behind how you created the dish, or some interesting nutritional facts about foods served in your establishment all help to maintain interest. It also gives you the opportunity as the executive chef to personally invite people to stop by and experience your signature fine dining.

Sous Chef Perhaps there is no bigger decision an executive chef has to make than selecting the proper sous chef. The sous chef ("sous" is French for "under") is the second-in-command. Reaching the level of sous chef is quite an accomplishment in the culinary field. This is where the best shine, and it is the final step before becoming an executive chef.

A good sous chef can take a great deal of the pressure off the head chef. With the top chef taking care of so many of the overall kitchen management issues, sous chefs who can run the day-to-day operations without a hitch are invaluable.

Sous chefs know the recipes used in the kitchen as well as the executive chefs do. Things are moving so fast in a kitchen at peak times that good sous chefs have to know all the recipes for all the dishes without taking the time to look at any written instructions.

If the executive chef makes any changes in a recipe or the cooking techniques used in the kitchen, it is up to the sous chef to inform the rest of the staff and demonstrate any changes. When the kitchen opens, it is the job of the sous chef to make sure all elements of the day's food preparations are covered, from chopping vegetables to mixing dressings and sauces.

As second-in-command, the sous chef has to have excellent organizational skills. Besides overseeing the cooking operation on a moment-to-moment basis, the sous chef makes sure all other kitchen staff members are doing their jobs. That means garbage is being bagged and disposed of properly, dishes are being washed, and linens are being collected. Under the watchful eye of the sous chef, the kitchen is completely cleaned at the end of the work day, all equipment and utensils are put away, and all food is stored properly. Sous chefs plan out the work for the day and give out daily assignments. They have to know all they can about the abilities of the station chefs they are working with and make assignments accordingly.

Station Chefs
The size of the restaurant and the number of customers usually dictate the number of station chefs on staff. The station chef, who reports directly to the sous chef, is in charge of one part of the kitchen and usually has a small staff of one or two assistants. A station chef may be in charge of one function or several, depending on the size of the restaurant operation.

One of the most important station chefs is the saucier. The saucier is an accomplished chef, and is often the third-in-command in the kitchen hierarchy. The saucier is charged with the responsibility of making all the sauces used on the various dishes on the menu, and there is normally a wide variety of sauces. Making any sauteed items is also the purview of this chef.

Other station chefs in the classical hierarchy established by Escoffier in France include:

Grillardin, the grill cook

Potager, the soup and stock cook

Rôtisseur, the cook responsible for roasted, broiled, and braised meats and their gravies, plus making meats to order

Friturier, the cook in charge of deep frying

Poissonnier, the cook who makes all the fish, including shellfish

Entremetier, the cook who prepares the vegetables and starches, including potatoes, rice, and sometimes pastas

Garde manger, the cook who handles all the cold foods, like salads and dressings, pates, and cold hors d'oeuvres.

Pastry Chef Most fine-dining kitchens have a pastry chef. Pastry chefs are specialists who make all the desserts. Pastry chefs work with the executive chef to decide what desserts perfectly complement the entrees. They compile a list of the ingredients they need to make the desserts and submit it to the executive chef for ordering. Pastry chefs also keep a running inventory of supplies, as they use them, so they never run short of any ingredients. Managing their own station in the kitchen, pastry chefs assemble their creations individually as orders come in.

*Chef instructing trainee in
restaurant kitchen.*

I Am a Sous Chef "When people ask me what it takes to do my job, I tell them you have to be able to multitask. I guess they expect me to say 'cook.' That goes without saying, but I don't think people realize how many tasks a sous chef has to do at one time. I oversee everything that is going on in the kitchen.

In a fine dining restaurant, as each order comes in, I make sure the line cooks know what is needed to complete that order. Multiply that by dozens of orders, many coming in at the same time.

An order may consist of several courses, including an appetizer, soup, entree, and dessert, and work on those courses has to be started at the right time. If the timing is off, guests can get the main course before they are done eating the appetizer or maybe a half-hour after they've eaten the appetizer. Neither is acceptable.

I make sure each of the dishes is prepared properly. Some dishes can be complicated to prepare. Our chefs have to follow the recipe that has been created by our executive chef. I inspect every dish to make sure it meets the executive chef's quality standards, and that the presentation on the plate is perfect. I instruct the waiters when to serve the dish, and make sure they know exactly which table and which guest gets each dish.

The kitchen is very busy, but that does not mean that it is disorganized. I make sure everything runs smoothly. To do that I get in about three or four hours before everyone else. I make sure the cooking stations are ready to go, which means they were left spotless after use the day before, and everything was put away in its proper place.

Cleanliness is my responsibility and should be taken seriously by any sous chef. If there is anything amiss, I take care of it. Meeting health code standards and going beyond them cannot be stressed enough. The reputation of everyone in the kitchen – not to mention the restaurant itself —depends on it.

I review the menu. In the restaurant I work in, the executive chef makes up the house menu, but I have a great deal of input on the specials. I do a daily inventory and make sure we have everything we need.

Prep work is very important to making an outstanding meal. I make sure our line cooks start their prep work on time – cutting vegetables, seasoning meats, making dressings. We just can't get behind in the prep work. It upsets the whole schedule.

I assign people different tasks, deploy chefs where they are needed, train new employees, and, during peak hours, I jump in and do some cooking myself.

Usually the executive chef will close up, but those extra hours a sous chef puts in before everyone else comes to work can make the difference between an easy or tough day in the kitchen."

I Am an Executive Chef and Owner of a White-Tablecloth Restaurant

"I think you have to have a high level of dedication to succeed in this business. You have to pay your dues, however, you can definitely make it to the top, because there is always room for the truly innovative and the very creative. Customers crave that and will pay for the chance to taste your creations. If you have something really important to contribute, you will break through.

This is one of the best times for new chefs to break in because there are so many places, including numerous cooking competitions, for up-and-coming chefs to display their talents. Television has helped with that. The media attention has made chefs celebrities and really brought attention to the career. The public is so aware of cooking and what makes good food. Don't let all that celebrity stuff fool you, however. You have to get in the trenches and do the real work. You'll be tested in the day-to-day fray, and you will have to produce consistently without the bright lights of the TV cameras and fawning interviewers.

That could mean being a station chef or a line cook for several years. It will entail extensive training before you get your big break. It could require serving as a sous chef for many years.

I worked those jobs before becoming an executive chef, and then I still took a chance leaving what I felt was a pretty secure job as a top chef to start my own restaurant – a very risky move. So add confidence in the mix because I felt I could offer my guests something very special, much different than they could get anywhere else, and that is how you have to feel to go out on your own.

I have two partners. I am the talent, and they take care of the business end of it. I have a little knowledge of the business side of a restaurant operation, enough to know what's going on and what is needed to stay afloat, but I stick to kitchen management and bringing in the customers with dishes only we can prepare – our exclusives. You must have reliable and knowledgeable business partners. That allows you to do what you do best – serve great food.

Once you have established a reputation, you have to maintain it. That goes for a chef who owns part of a restaurant as well as a chef who works for someone else. The people don't keep coming in because you used to serve great dishes. You have to keep it cutting-edge, exciting, and fresh.

I look at it this way. I want to make our food the attraction for the evening. I want our food to be the event, the reason people go out. So that wow factor has to be there day in and day out."

I Am a Pastry Chef "Good pastry chefs should know all there is about baking and making desserts, but that doesn't mean they cannot prepare a main course, and I have on a number of occasions. I have often been asked to step in when another chef has been unable to show up for work.

I have worked at several upscale restaurants and all of them prided themselves on the desserts they served. That means their desserts had to be distinctive. I've always felt I was free to use a great deal of creativity in my job because of that.

I am challenged to make something very special. At the same time, this job requires precision and skill. It is so easy to make a dessert that is too rich, over the top. It's a balancing act, and you have to be in control. I believe a bad dessert can ruin a whole meal, and the entire dining experience with it. So it's my job to make sure that doesn't happen.

I chose to be a pastry chef because the pace is a bit slower than what other chefs have to deal with, and I like that. One reason is that restaurants do not offer as many desserts as they do main courses. Usually there are only five or six desserts on the menu.

Also, many components of a dessert are made ahead of time. You don't start baking a cake or making whipped cream when a customer orders dessert. You just have to put everything together. Don't get me wrong: everything is made fresh and usually that day. I make everything from scratch.

Desserts cover a lot of ground. They can be rather complex. Fillings, sauces, ice cream, fondant, puddings, cookies, meringues, mousses, custards, crusts, crepes – anything that goes into a dessert, I make it all myself –

nothing comes out of a package. That takes time, so I start my day a bit earlier than other chefs.

Desserts are often seasonal. There are some that are expected, like creme brulee and tiramisu. Do we have those on that menu or not? Do we go with the unexpected instead? Decisions have to be made.

Pastry chefs do have to know how to bake breads, but I rarely do that in my job. If the owners of an upscale restaurant want bread made fresh every day, they will usually bring in a baker to do that and leave the pastry chef to concentrate on desserts.

Not all pastry chefs work in restaurants. I know some accomplished pastry chefs who have started upscale pastry shops, even dessert-only establishments. These places are very trendy and offer a different kind of fare, a real treat."

PERSONAL QUALIFICATIONS

EVERYONE KNOWS A CHEF HAS TO BE A GREAT COOK, BUT that is just part of what it takes to earn respect in the kitchen. Creativity is the magic ingredient. Giving an old standard, like beef bourguignon, a fantastic new flavor impresses diners. Bringing exotic new foods to the menu captivates patrons and keeps them returning for more. New ideas have to flow from your imagination.

Your talent for handling everything that goes on behind the scenes is what makes you as successful as the meals you serve. Whether you are an executive chef or a station chef in charge of just one part of the kitchen, you have to stay unruffled and undeterred under intense pressure. There is so much going on in a busy kitchen, and it is up to you to stay calm and keep those around you focused on the job at hand. Panic is not in your vocabulary, as you thrive on the nonstop action of preparing one scrumptious dish after another and solving any problems that come along in between.

Doing several tasks at one time has to come naturally to chefs, since they rarely handle only one assignment at a time. That means being very organized and having a game plan to manage things when the kitchen becomes the eye of the storm.

Good communications keep everything running smoothly. Top chefs know how and when to address their staffs. There cannot be any guesswork. The entire kitchen staff has to be on the same page and all the chefs on duty have to be aware of their mission at all times.

There may be dietary considerations and dishes that have to be prepared a certain way with no room for error. Your leadership abilities will be tested all the time, and your confidence will be on display whenever you pick up a spatula or a spoon.

Being able to spot another person with exceptional culinary talent is a gift any good chef must possess. Successful chefs surround themselves with other good cooks. They know the key to success is teamwork, so building that team is a vital part of the job. All personnel have to work together, do their jobs, and pull for the team as a whole. Most executive chefs hire the assistant chefs who work by their side. Those chefs in turn hire the cooking staff who work with them, so having a knack for spotting good people with culinary savvy is important for chefs working on all levels.

Cooking is often a numbers game, so chefs need a good working knowledge of mathematics in order to increase and decrease ingredients in recipes, depending on portion size. Ingredients must be measured precisely or it could compromise the taste of a dish. Chefs must also be able to calculate the cost of each dish, including preparation. It is the basis used for charging customers.

ATTRACTIVE FEATURES

MOST CHEFS CANNOT WAIT TO GET TO work and start filling empty plates with their culinary creations. When you are in the kitchen, you can fire up your imagination every day. This is not a routine desk job. It never gets boring in the world of mixing bowls and cutting boards.

The occasional downtime can be used to whip up a daring new sauce or salad dressing. You come up with different specials. There is always something stirring in the kitchen – that is what makes it such an exciting place to work.

This is a field where you are constantly changing, evolving, experimenting, and growing. Small plates, spa food, wraps, panini, vegan – what will be the next food trend? Will you be the one who starts it? When it comes to cooking, it has not all been done before, and foodies are always ripe for the latest taste sensation.

Though chefs usually start out at the bottom rung in the kitchen, the chance for growth is unlimited. Many chefs rise through the ranks and end up running their own kitchens, and sometimes also owning their own restaurants.

Hard work pays off in this field. If you like learning new things, this is definitely the job for you. There is constant breaking news in the cooking industry, and it is not just about different foods. The reports cover everything from the latest kitchen gadgets to healthier ways of preparing meals, recently passed public health regulations to innovative ways to store food to avoid waste.

Chefs learn from each other, and while the field may be competitive, you will also find a great deal of camaraderie and an open exchange of ideas. Perhaps you will never have a greater competitor than yourself. Chefs want to outdo themselves every day, trying to make the meals they prepare as memorable for customers as they possibly can be.

As you build your reputation, you also set the stage for higher earnings. Four-star restaurants want top chefs and they are willing to pay for talent. Top chefs are riding a wave of popularity that seems to be increasing daily as the media focuses more and more attention on these stars of the kitchen.

What an experience! Walking into your dining room and seeing people enjoying the food you made. You know you have put in a good day's work and, for many of these customers, you have even exceeded expectations. Tomorrow you get a chance to do it again.

UNATTRACTIVE FEATURES

CHEFS RARELY SIT DOWN AND HAVE dinner with their families. That's because they are usually working when most people are having dinner. This schedule can take a toll on family life. You may become a stranger to your children. Early mornings, late nights, weekends, holidays – almost any time others are not working, you are – visiting the local fish market at dawn, firing up the ovens before the line cooks start grilling, or turning off the lights after the last patron has said good night. These odd hours are something you have to be comfortable with going into the profession. The hours are long too. Some days, like Saturday, may be nonstop, no breaks. It is not uncommon to put in 50, even 60-hour workweeks.

Being a chef will be your life. Those who choose this career are very committed to it. The pressure won't let up. No matter how adept you get at cooking even the most difficult dishes, you will always be working under a deadline. Getting food out to customers perfectly timed goes with the territory. Though some nights will be busier than others, you will probably never have as much time as you like to do your job.

There is little room for error. Customers are paying their money for a great meal, and they expect to get it. If food is not prepared properly, it is sent back, and it either has to be corrected or redone from scratch. That can result in a waste of both time and food. It can also result in a customer who vows never to return.

You will spend most of your time on your feet. It might not seem like it, but being a chef is a physically demanding job. In busy kitchens, you always run the risk of incurring an injury. You are working around fire and fast-moving sharp objects. You will be dealing with your share of burns, cuts, and nicks.

The kitchen may be small and hard to maneuver in. This can make for difficult working conditions. Some of the finest restaurants in the world have kitchens far smaller than the dining rooms. Kitchens can also be noisy, smelly, and hot. You will not find much peace and quiet, wearing an apron and a toque (traditional tall white chef's hat).

EDUCATION AND TRAINING

THERE ARE MANY DIFFERENT PATHS to learning how to be a great chef.

On-the-job training

The traditional path to becoming a chef is learning on the job. Of course, you have to possess some cooking ability and a love of working with food before you step into a professional kitchen. Then, on the job, you are taught by experts the intricacies of making exceptional meals. Aspiring chefs start out at the beginner level, chopping vegetables and preparing ingredients, and work up from there. Chefs-in-training are mentored for years by accomplished, often renowned chefs, and the instruction is hands-on in real-time restaurant kitchens.

The learning is fast and furious, and you get a chance to witness every aspect of life in the kitchen, from cooking to ordering inventory. You pick up shortcuts and learn how to present the finished dishes.

Many of these on-the-job training experiences offer the added bonus of bringing home a paycheck. The experience you get looks great on a résumé, and there is room for advancement.

Culinary Schools

Another route that is more common today is formal schooling. Culinary schools are very popular now and provide insights into the career that you might not have time to get when you are pushed right into the workforce. Among those are the history and culture behind the dishes you are preparing, and the opportunity to specialize in ethnic dishes, special dietary restrictions, and other niches. You can take the time to perfect your baking skills, or focus on the many ways to prepare sauces.

Some culinary schools offer both four-year bachelor's degrees and two-year associate degrees. Others offer certificates in certain specialties. To decide on the right path, you have to have a clear sense of what you are trying to accomplish and find the school that will meet your needs. Learn about each school's faculty, facilities, curriculum, and accreditation. Get all the available information about tuition and financial aid.

Culinary schools are located all over the country. One well-known culinary school is the Culinary Institute of America (CIA). This school offers both associate and bachelor's degrees. The CIA has US campuses in Hyde Park, New York; St. Helena, California; and San Antonio, Texas. Courses in every aspect of the cooking profession are offered at the institute.

The growing number of culinary schools that offer programs and courses in cooking, baking, and restaurant management include:

- New England Culinary Institute in Montpelier, Vermont
- The International Culinary Center (formerly French Culinary Institute) in New York City
- Lincoln Culinary Institute in West Palm Beach

➡️L'Ecole Culinaire in Memphis and St. Louis

Le Cordon Bleu is the largest hospitality education institution in the world, with 18 schools in the United States, and 35 worldwide. The school has a wide range of cooking courses. The original Cordon Bleu cooking school was founded in Paris in 1895, and these schools are the modern version of that legendary institution.

Colleges

There are colleges that offer culinary training and degrees as well. Kendall College in Chicago offers associate degrees in baking and pastry art, plus culinary art. The school also has a bachelor's program in culinary art.

Johnson and Wales University in Providence, Rhode Island has two-year degree programs in food service management, culinary art, and baking and pastry art. The school also offers a bachelor's degree program in culinary nutrition, culinary art, and baking and pastry art.

Community Colleges

The list of community colleges that offer associate degrees in the culinary arts continues to grow and includes Finger Lakes Community College in Canandaigua, New York; Metropolitan Community College in Omaha, Nebraska; and Spokane Community College in the state of Washington.

Community colleges have become a good way of acquiring culinary skills at a reasonable cost and in a relatively short period. Degrees from these colleges are respected in the food industry.

Certifications

Certifications are awarded by professional groups like the American Culinary Federation (ACF), the American Bakers Association, and the United States Chef Association. Chefs have to meet rigorous professional standards to get these certifications, which are held in high esteem among chefs throughout the field.

EARNINGS

YOUR SALARY WILL DEPEND ON THE type of restaurant you work for and the level of job you hold in the kitchen. The greater your responsibility, the higher your income. In addition, the more exclusive and expensive the restaurant, the better the pay. Your experience, educational background, certifications, reputation, and the demand for your services all figure in your annual salary.

Line cooks usually start out at an hourly rate of $10 to $15, or a yearly salary in the range of $26,000 to $29,000.

Station chefs make between $40,000 and $45,000 a year.

Pastry chefs command salaries in the $50,000 range, with an executive pastry chef making about $70,000.

Sous chefs can earn between $70,000 and $80,000, with an executive chef paid on average $100,000 to $125,000 per year.

Top chefs can earn even more with cookbook deals, television appearances, and teaching opportunities. Sous chefs and pastry chefs can also bring in some extra money by teaching and making appearances.

Another income stream for executive chefs is endorsements. Many chefs lend their names and backing to all types of kitchen equipment and utensils. Some chefs market their own kitchen inventions and packaged products, such as sauces and dips.

Chefs who own their own restaurants receive whatever profit the operation makes on an annual basis, after paying all expenses – salaries, rent, interest on loans, food ingredients, utilities, etc. Usually a large capital investment is required to build a new restaurant or buy an existing facility. Partners may be required to invest money up front, and they are usually paid a return based on the operating profits. Owners of very successful restaurants, which can often spawn chains of restaurants, can make millions. A typical arrangement is two partners owning a restaurant – the chef in the kitchen, and a business person in charge of the "front of the house" functions, including all office and business aspects of the restaurant, human resources, financial and taxation.

OPPORTUNITIES

THERE ARE EMPLOYMENT OPPORTUNITIes for chefs all over the world. You will not be limited to one country or one region, especially if you are willing to travel and relocate.

Finding a job might mean using your imagination and exploring possibilities. Chefs work in many places besides the traditional full-service restaurant. For example, many large fast-food chains have chefs working for them as consultants in their headquarters kitchens, creating menus, recipes, and cooking methods for their franchises. Chefs today are very knowledgeable about caloric intake, nutrition facts, and healthy diets. In this increasingly health-conscious society, all eateries, including fast food chains, want to include healthy choices on their menus.

The travel and tourism industry is the largest employer in the world, and many chefs are employed in hotels and resorts throughout the world. Every time a new hotel opens up, especially in a vacation destination, there is at least one restaurant – often several – and that means jobs for people with culinary expertise. Tourist attractions also include places to eat, often with special menus to enhance the visitor experience, featuring local produce or regional specialties.

The catering industry offers a wealth of jobs for chefs, an especially likely place for young chefs to start their careers. Caterers provide both on-site and off-site services. Besides those big events, like retirement dinners and gala grand openings, caterers have clients that use their services on a daily basis. Airlines, hospitals, and schools often retain the services of caterers who employ chefs to plan menus and prepare meals. These institutional catering operations are usually owned by large companies, and what makes them attractive to people starting out in the culinary industry is that they have a stable roster of clients and can offer a good starting salary and benefits. This is referred to in the business as "volume cooking." While volume cooking is usually based on the specifications of the client, there are those times, like holidays and special occasions, when you can tap into your own creativity. Being a chef in an institutional catering operation gives you a broad exposure to the food industry.

Another growth area in food service that presents opportunities for chefs is home meal replacement. Offered by many retail food markets, these finely prepared carry-out meals help busy professionals put nutritional meals on the table without having to take the time to prepare them themselves. These restaurant-quality meals may include entrees, side dishes, salads, and desserts that are packaged to take home. The meals are prepared by skilled chefs using top ingredients. These options are enjoying increasing popularity in today's busy world.

GETTING STARTED

MANY OF THE GREAT CHEFS GOT THEIR start by serving as an apprentice. Having never forgotten that experience, they are usually willing to offer the same opportunity for others just beginning in the culinary field.

Openings for apprentice chefs are plentiful – not just in the United States, but all over the world. Chefs train for years to master the subtle nuances of flavors that combine to make the perfect dish. Many aspiring chefs welcome the chance to take an apprenticeship in a foreign country and learn about preparing foods based in other ethnic cuisines. One of the top destinations is France, where great cooking is legendary and many great chefs got their start. Some young chefs do apprenticeships in several different countries before entering the job market.

Being exposed to foods of diverse cultures can give a chef an edge in the job market. You learn how to prepare these foods the way it is done in the native lands. Drawing on this knowledge, you can work in the kitchens of restaurants that serve these exotic delicacies. If you want to work in large metropolitan areas, this increases your options.

Some apprentice positions come with a paycheck; others do not. The duties of an apprentice change from day to day, and you get a chance to work with all the chefs in a restaurant kitchen and learn about the jobs they do. By taking on several apprenticeships, you get the opportunity to see how various kitchens are run under real-life conditions. Everything you studied in school will unfold before you. This will be a good time to decide if you want to specialize, developing a career in a niche area, like becoming a pastry or dessert chef.

You can make connections while serving as an apprentice. Networking is an important part of becoming a successful chef. The people you meet in kitchens around the world while you are perfecting your craft may be able to help you get a job. The same is true of the people you meet in culinary classes and schools. Making solid contacts can help you get interviews for positions you may otherwise not even know are available.

Starting at the bottom is one reality that everyone who enters the culinary field must accept. Though all chefs aspire to be chief or executive chef, that is not going to happen immediately. Most people will start out as a line chef and work their way up from there.

ASSOCIATIONS

- **Professional Chefs Association**
  www.professionalchef.com

- **World Association of Chef Societies (WACS)**
  http://www.wacs2000.org
  /wacs2010/en/main/index.php

- **American Culinary Federation (ACF)**
  www.acfchefs.org

- **United States Chef Association (USCA)**
  www.uschefassoc.com

- **International Association of Culinary Professionals (IACP)**
  www.iacp.com

- **United States Personal Chef Association**
  www.uspca.com

- **American Personal and Private Chef Association**
  www.personalchef.com

- **The Bread Bakers Guild of America**
  www.bbga.org

- **National Restaurant Association**
  www.restaurant.org

PUBLICATIONS

- Chef Magazine

- Worldchefs Magazine

- Saveur

- Art Culinaire

- Personal Chef Magazine

- Nation's Restaurant News

- The National Culinary Review

- Sizzle

- The Culinary Insider

- Restaurant Hospitality Magazine

- Super Chef

- Culinary Trends

- Global Chefs

WEBSITES

- **Research Chefs Association**
  www.culinology.com

- **World Master Chefs Society**
  www.worldmasterchefs.com

- **New York Women's Culinary Alliance (NYWCA)**
  www.nywca.org

- **Careers Through Culinary Arts Program**
  www.ccapinc.org/index.php

- **The American Institute of Wine & Food (AIWF)**
  www.aiwf.org

- **Women Chefs & Restaurateurs**
  www.womenchefs.org

- **The Association of Pastry Chefs**
  www.associationofpastrychefs
  .org

SCHOOLS

- **Culinary Institute of America (CIA)**
  http://www.ciachef.edu

- **New England Culinary Institute in Montpelier, Vermont**
  http://www.neci.edu

- **The International Culinary Center (formerly French Culinary Institute) in New York City**
  www.internationalculinarycenter
  .com

- **Lincoln Culinary Institute in West Palm Beach**
  http://www.lincolnedu.com
  /careers/culinary

- **L'Ecole Culinaire in Memphis and St. Louis**
  http://www.lecole.edu

- **Le Cordon Bleu**
  http://www.cordonbleuusa.com
  /home/en

- **Kendall College in Chicago**
  http://culinary.kendall.edu

- **Johnson and Wales University in Providence, Rhode Island**
  http://www.jwu.edu/college.aspx
  ?id=19888

- **Finger Lakes Community College in Canandaigua, New York**
  http://www.flcc.edu/academics
  /culinary/index.cfm

- **Metropolitan Community College in Omaha Nebraska**
  http://www.mccneb.edu/chrm
  /cculinaryartsandmanagement.asp

- **Spokane Community College in Washington**
  http://www.scc.spokane.edu

Made in the USA
Lexington, KY
21 March 2015